Bentley and the Giant Carrot

Written by

Lorinda DePeal Martin

Illustrated by

Cynthia Shubert

Dedication

In honor of my husband who is adored by our grandchildren and has our children's and my utmost respect.

And especially for Ansley, Emersyn, Camden, Joycelyn, Sadie, and Lucas the youngest half of our grands.

In Hopsville, there lived a kind old rabbit of many years named Bentley. His gray coat and silver whiskers were the only indication of his age, for he was as spry as the day he was born.

Bentley was also the bravest rabbit in Hopsville. He guarded the village and the Grand Garden, that stretched out the entire length of the town. Daily he made his rounds through the lookout tunnels to peak out the holes and watch for Red Fox.

The Grand Garden was planned by the bunny counsel after an incident that involved Bentley's uncle Laramie.

There was a monument at the center of the garden, in memory of Laramie, who was caught eating Farmer John's cabbage and never heard from again.

Rumor had it that Farmer John's wife had made a lovely meat pie that same afternoon. The Counsel had decided to plant a garden to supply all the veggies for Hopsville so that no other bunnies would end up missing.

By the outer edge of the garden near Bentley's home, there grew a giant carrot.

The giant carrot was the first thing that Red Fox passed as he came out of Trellis Woods each day hunting for bunnies.

Bentley was always ready for Red. The moment he caught sight of his red fur he would pull the cord in the tunnel to sound an alarm at each home.

When the bunnies heard the bell, they knew that they needed to hide quickly. Danger lurked about, and that danger's name was Red Fox. The bunnies had all stayed safe with Bentley as Hopsville's guard.

But poor Red had to stick to eating wild grapes for every meal! Grapes were his favorite, but he often craved rabbit stew.

Bentley took pride in being Hopsville's protector. However, what he loved more than that, was when the smallest bunnies visited him. At the end of each day, bunnies made their way to Bentley's to play games and listen to stories of long ago.

Their favorite stories were of the Carrot Festivals in the old days before Red Fox came to Hopsville.

The bunnies marveled at the giant carrot that was in Bentley's end of Grand Garden. Its orange top was as round as the oldest oak in Trellis Woods, and its green stalks shaded Bentley's home. The bunnies would ask how it came to grow so big, and Bentley, although he knew better, would say, with a twinkle in his eye, that it was magic that made it so big.

One day Bentley had been
to a party for his cousin
Jeremy's birthday. It was a
grand celebration!   There was
carrot cake, clover candy, and
lots of music.

He had taken a piece of
carrot cake home with him

and ate it with his lunch the following afternoon. His paws were sticky when he finished eating.

The cake reminded him of a song he had heard at the party, and he began humming the tune.

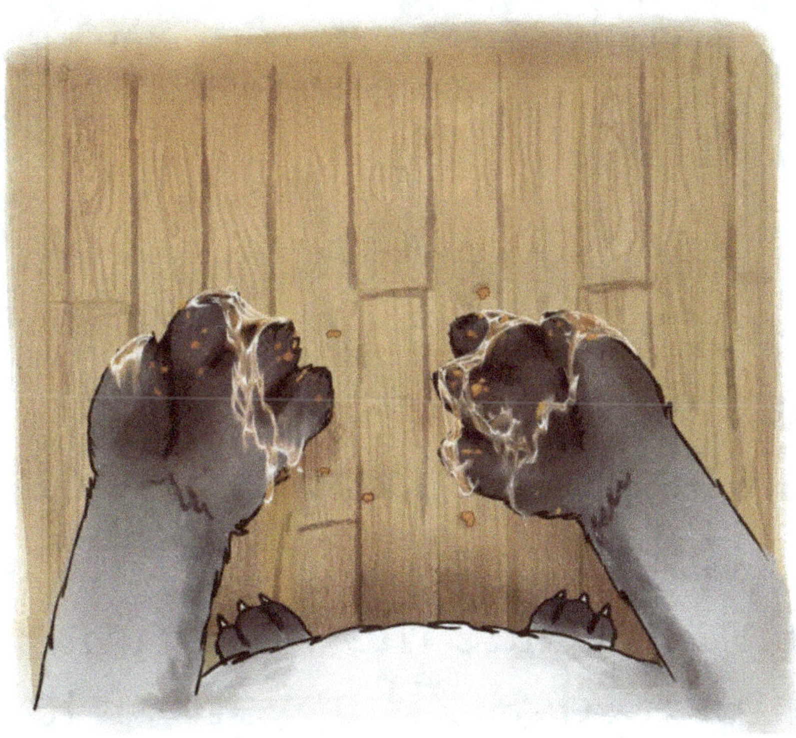

Bentley decided to slip down to Bubbling Brook in the meadow next to Trellis Woods to wash the sticky off.

Continuing to hum, Bentley made his way to the water's edge. The water felt great on this hot, August day as he eased his paws into the stream.

The sound of the water and Bentley's humming were so loud that he did not hear Red Fox sneak up behind.

Red pounced upon Bentley, capturing him in a single bound.

"I caught you!" exclaimed Red Fox.

Bentley couldn't believe this could happen. Not to Hopsville's best guard!

Bentley's pride was hurt. He had to think quick before Red Fox made a meal of him.

First, he pleaded for Red to let him go, but Red Fox was relentless. Bentley's heart raced. What was he to do?

Then he remembered how his cousin once talked his way out of a problem with another fox, tricking him into throwing him into the briers. Perhaps he could outsmart him.

"Oh, you have got me now. It is too bad that my secret will die with me," said Bentley.

"What secret is that?" Red asked.

"Why, my secret for growing large fruits and vegetables. Have you not seen the giant carrot outside my home?" Bentley replied.

"Why yes, I know of the giant carrot, I pass it every day," replied Red.

He agreed to let loose of Bentley in exchange for the secret of growing large fruits and vegetables.

Now, Red loved fruit, especially wild grapes, and his mouth watered at the thought of grapes as large as the giant carrot.

As he followed Bentley to the giant carrot, his thoughts shifted from giant grapes to rabbit stew.

Bentley hurried along.
Seeing the gleam in Red's
eyes and the way that he
licked his lips.

Arriving at Bentley's end of the garden, Bentley told Red Fox,

"First, you must dig a big hole beside the carrot so that you will have plenty of this magic soil to grow your grapes in."

"So that is it, the secret is just the soil," said Red. He thought that he might go ahead and eat Bentley, then worry about planting grapes later.

Bentley sensed that Red was becoming impatient and quickly added:

"Oh, but that is just the first part. I will tell you the rest after you dig the hole."

Red dug a large hole beside the carrot. Bentley looked it over and said,

"Well, that is a fine hole, but that is only enough special soil for small grapes."

Red fox continued digging the hole deeper and broader beside the giant carrot, and Bentley continued to comment that he still did not have enough of the magic soil for large grapes.

Suddenly, the earth began to tremble. Red Fox was knocked off his feet at the bottom of the hole. Bentley, who was standing at the edge of the breach, was knocked back as the giant carrot came crashing down on Red Fox.

All over Hopsville, the
ground had shaken. The

thundering crash sent
bunnies diving into their
homes, shaking with fear.

All went silent. Everyone listened intently. Soon they heard Bentley crying out to them,

"Everyone, come see! Come see! Hurry, look at what has happened!"

The giant carrot has fallen on Red Fox and has squashed him flat!

The mayor of Hopsville
declared a special holiday in
honor of Bentley. The citizens
of Hopsville gathered for the
largest carrot festival in the
history of their town. All day,

and into the evening everyone celebrated until slowly The crowd dwindled down.

As the festival ended, the youngest bunnies plead for Bentley to tell them a story

Bentley decided to share a story about a carrot that stayed in the ground, season after season, due to a pesky fox.

The carrot finally became so large that it was too big to be harvested. Bentley paused and that familiar twinkle returned to his eyes, "Without a bit of magic," he added.

The End